MUTT

MUGS

(and posh pups too)

Karen Prince

Hylas Publishing
Publisher: Sean Moore
Creative Director: Karen Prince
Designer: Pakpoom Rojanapisit
Editor: Mie Kingsley
Proofreader: Ginger Skinner

First published by
Hylas Publishing
129 Main Street, Irvington,
New York 10533
www.hylaspublishing.com

Compilation Copyright © Hylas Publishing 2004
Library of Congress Data available upon request

ISBN 1-59258-108-0

Set in News701 BT and Snell Special Script
Printed and bound in Hong Kong

Distributed in the U.S.A. by the National Book Network
and in Canada by Kate Walker & Company

2   4   6   8   10   9   7   5   3   1

MUTT

MUGS

www.hylaspublishing.com

HYLAS

"Reverence: the spiritual
attitude of a man to a god
and a dog to a man."

Ambrose Bierce

"Dog: A kind of additional
or subsidiary Deity designed
to catch the overflow
and surplus of the
world's worship."

Ambrose Bierce

"A good dog
deserves
a good bone."

Ben Johnson

"Every dog
is a lion
at home."

"Scratch a dog
and you'll find
a permanent job."

Franklin P. Jones

"Our dog chases
people on a bike.
We've had to take
it off him."

Winston Churchill

"A dog is the only
thing on earth
that loves you
more than you
love yourself."

Josh Billings

"Money will
buy a pretty good
dog, but it won't buy
the wag of his tail."

Josh Billings

"The great pleasure of a dog
is that you may make a fool
of yourself with him and not only
will he not scold you, but he will
make a fool of himself too."

Samuel Butler

"Outside of a dog,
a book is a man's
best friend. Inside a dog,
it's too dark to read."

Groucho Marx

"A dog teaches
a boy fidelity,
perseverance,
and to turn around
three times before
lying down."

Robert Benchley

"He cannot
be a gentleman
which loveth
not a dog."

John Northbrooke

"No one appreciates the
very special genius of your
conversation as a dog does."

Christopher Morley

"The dog is man's best friend.

He has a tail on one end.

Up in front he has teeth.

And four legs underneath."

Ogden Nash

"A dog
has the soul
of a philosopher."

Plato

"When most
of us talk to our
dogs, we tend
to forget they're
not people."

Julia Glass

"It is fatal to let any dog
know that he is funny,
for he immediately loses
his head and starts
hamming it up."

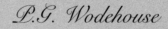

"Children and dogs

are as necessary

to the welfare

of the country

as Wall Street

and the railroads."

Harry S. Truman

"Living with
a dog is easy
—like living with
an idealist."

H.L. Mencken

"There is no
psychiatrist
in the world like
a puppy licking
your face."

Ben Williams

"You can say any fool thing
to a dog, and the dog will give
you this look that says,
'My God, you're RIGHT!
I NEVER would've
thought of that!'"

Dave Barry

"A really companionable
and indispensable dog
is an accident of nature.
You can't get it by breeding
for it, and you can't
buy it with money.
It just happens along."

E.B. White

"The best
thing about
a man
is his dog."

Proverb

"Acquiring a dog

may be the

only opportunity

a human ever has

to choose a relative."

Mordecai Siegal

"Dogs have given us their
absolute all. We are the center
of their universe. We are the focus
of their love and faith and trust.
They serve us in return for scraps.
It is without a doubt the best
deal man has ever made."

"He is your friend, your partner, your defender, your dog. You are his life, his love, his leader. He will be yours, faithful and true, to the last beat of his heart. You owe it to him to be worthy of such devotion."

Unknown

"It's not the size
of the dog in the fight,
it's the size of the
fight in the dog."

Mark Twain

"To err
is human;
to forgive,
canine."

Anonymous

"Whoever said
'let sleeping
dogs lie' didn't
sleep with dogs."

Unknown

"Dogs are our link to paradise.
They don't know evil or jealousy
or discontent. To sit with a dog
on a hillside on a glorious
afternoon is to be back
in Eden, where doing nothing
was not boring—it was peace."

Milan Kundera

"Whoever said
you can't buy
happiness forgot
little puppies."

Gene Hill

"The more
I know about
men, the more
I like dogs."

Gloria Allred

"The one absolutely unselfish
friend that man can have
in this selfish world, the one that
never deserts him, the one that
never proves ungrateful
or treacherous, is his dog. . .
He will kiss the hand that has
no food to offer; he will lick
the wounds and sores that come
in encounter with the roughness
of the world. . . .When all other
friends desert, he remains."

George G. Vest

"I'm a lean dog, a keen dog,

a wild dog, and lone;

I'm a rough dog, a tough dog,

hunting on my own;

I'm a bad dog, a mad dog,

teasing silly sheep;

I love to sit and bay the moon

to keep fat souls from sleep."

Irene MacLeod

"Every dog

has his day."

Miguel de Cervantes

"The dog
was created
specially
for children.
He is the god
of frolic."

Henry W. Beecher

"I've caught more ills from people sneezing over me and giving me virus infections than from kissing dogs."

Barbara Woodhouse

"Why, that dog is practically
a Phi Beta Kappa. She can
sit up and beg, and she
can give her paw—I don't
say she will, but she can."

Dorothy Parker

"Love me,

love my dog."

Saint Bernard

"To a dog, the
whole world
is a smell."

Anonymous

"From the dog's point of view,
his master is an elongated
and abnormally cunning dog."

Mabel L. Robinson

"There is no faith which
has never yet been broken,
except that of a truly
faithful dog."

Konrad Lorenz

"Some days you're the dog, some days you're the hydrant."

Unknown

"The biggest
dog has
been a pup."

Joaquin Miller

"They are better
than human beings
because they know
but do not tell."

Emily Dickinson

"Agreeable friends—they
ask no questions, they
pass no criticisms."

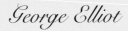

"My dog is half
pit bull, half
poodle. Not much
of a watchdog, but
a vicious gossip!"

Craig Shoemaker

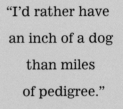

"I'd rather have
an inch of a dog
than miles
of pedigree."

Dana Burnet

"Buy a pup and your
money will buy
love unflinching."

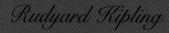

"All knowledge,

the totality

of all questions

and all answers,

is contained

in the dog."

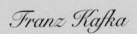

"My little dog—
a heartbeat
at my feet."

Edith Wharton

"Dogs are not
our whole life,
but they make
our lives whole."

Roger Caras

"All trees have bark.
All dogs bark. Therefore,
all dogs are trees.
The fallacy of barking
up the wrong tree."

Unknown

"If a dog's prayers
were answered,
bones would
rain from the sky."

"It's funny how dogs
and cats know
the inside of folks
better than
other folks do."

Eleanor H. Potter

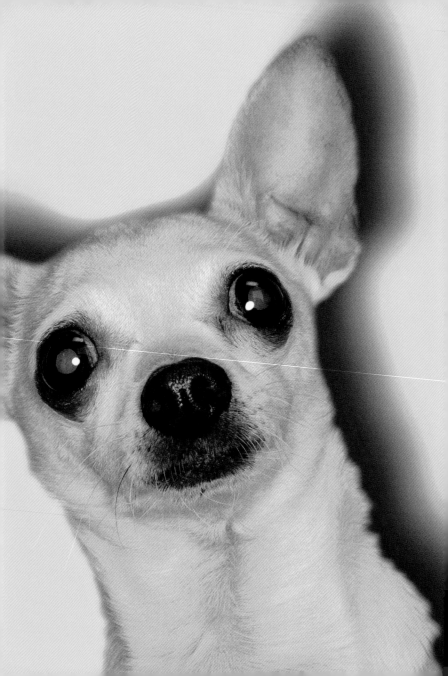

"I am I because
my little dog
knows me."

Gertrude Stein

"A man may smile

and bid you hail,

yet wish you to the devil;

but when a good dog wags

his tail, you know

he's on the level."

Anonymous

"The reason a dog
has so many friends
is that he wags his tail
instead of his tongue."

Anonymous

PICTURE CREDITS